W9-CHD-930

FLAMINGOS

Jennifer McDougall

Grolier
an imprint of

📖 SCHOLASTIC

www.scholastic.com/librarypublishing

Published 2009 by Grolier
An imprint of Scholastic Library Publishing
Old Sherman Turnpike, Danbury,
Connecticut 06816

For The Brown Reference Group plc
Project Editor: Jolyon Goddard
Picture Researcher: Clare Newman
Designers: Dave Allen, Jeni Child, Lynne Ross,
John Dinsdale, Sarah Williams
Managing Editors: Bridget Giles, Tim Harris

Volume ISBN-13: 978-0-7172-6293-9
Volume ISBN-10: 0-7172-6293-6

**Library of Congress
Cataloging-in-Publication Data**

Nature's children. Set 4.
    p. cm.
    Includes bibliographical references and
    index.
    ISBN 13: 978-0-7172-8083-4
    ISBN 10: 0-7172-8083-7 ((set 4) : alk. paper)
    1. Animals--Encyclopedias, Juvenile. 1.
    Grolier (Firm)
    QL49.N385 2009
    590.3--dc22
                                2007046315

Printed and bound in China

PICTURE CREDITS

Front Cover: **Shutterstock**: Marina Cano
Truba.

Back Cover: **FLPA**: Pete Oxford/Minden
Pictures; **Photolibrary.com**: Kerstin Layer;
Shutterstock: Steffen Foerster Photography,
Ian Stewart.

Ardea: Leslie Brown 45; **Nature PL**:
George McCarthy 18, Pete Oxford 42, Solvin
Zankl 41; **Photolibrary.com**: Daniel Cox
37, David M. Dennis 29, Juniors Bildarchiv 34,
Barbara Von Huffmann 33; **Shutterstock**:
Sebastien Burel 21, Eric Gevaert 38, Jenny
Horne 4, Chad Littlejohn 5, Stephen Meese
13, Antonio Jorge Nunes 10, Alan Othnay 17,
Hashim Pudiyapura 14, Lori Skelton 22,
Steffen Foerster Photography 2–3, 26–27, 30,
Johan Swanepoel 6, Rick Thornton 9; **Still
Pictures**: H. O. Schulze/Wildlife 46.

Contents

FACT FILE: Flamingos

Class	Birds (Aves)
Order	Flamingos (Phoenicopteriformes)
Family	Phoenicopteridae
Genera	*Phoenicopterus, Phoeniconaias,* and *Phoenicoparrus*
Species	Andean flamingo, Chilean flamingo, James's flamingo, greater flamingo, and lesser flamingo
World distribution	Southern Europe and Asia, Africa, Mexico, South America, Caribbean, and the Galápagos Islands
Habitat	Inland lakes, marshes, lagoons, mangrove swamps, and mud flats near the sea
Distinctive physical characteristics	Tall birds with long neck and legs, pink feathers, and a bent pink and black beak
Habits	Flamingos live in big flocks or colonies; they often fly at night to avoid predators; they feed their young on "milk"
Diet	Small animals and other living things in the water

Introduction

Flamingos are among the most easily recognized birds. They have beautiful pink **plumage** and a large downward-pointing beak. They are often seen balancing effortlessly on one leg in the shallow lakes or coastal regions where they live. But there is much more to flamingos than just their appearance. They live in flocks of up to many thousands of birds. They feed by dipping their head underwater and using their beak to sift tiny living things out of the water. Flamingos build a nest out of mud. They even feed their young, or **chick**, on a type of milk!

The bend halfway down a flamingo's leg is actually the bird's ankle!

5

The Caribbean flamingo is also known as the rosy or American flamingo. It is the only type of flamingo that lives naturally in North America.

6

Five in the Family

The flamingo family contains five **species**, or types, of flamingos. They live in various parts of the world.

The most widespread member of the family is the greater flamingo. There are two distinct kinds of the greater flamingo. One kind lives in Africa, southern and southwestern Asia, and southern Europe. The other kind, known as the Caribbean flamingo, is found in the Caribbean, Galápagos Islands, Mexico, and on the coasts of Venezuela and Colombia.

The lesser flamingo is the most common flamingo. It is found in Africa and Asia, and occasionally flies to southern Europe.

The other three species live only in South America. The Chilean flamingo lives along the Andes Mountains, from Peru and Uruguay down to the southern tip of South America. The Andean flamingo and James's flamingo are very closely related. They both live high up in the salt lakes of Peru, Bolivia, Argentina, and Chile.

Meet the Relatives

Scientists are puzzled about which birds are the flamingos' closest relatives. Flamingos are very distinct, different from all other types of birds. But they do share some similarities with other groups of birds.

Some scientists believe that the flamingos' closest relatives are storks and ibises (I-BIS-SIZ), which have a body shape and bones similar to those of flamingos. Other scientists believe that flamingos are more closely related to waterbirds, such as ducks, geese, and swans. Flamingo chicks behave in a similar way to young waterbirds, and both groups have webbed feet.

Recent evidence gathered from the use of new technology suggests that a group of birds called grebes (GREEBZ) are flamingos' closest living relatives—although the two groups of birds do not look very similar. Until further proof is found, scientists are still unsure where exactly flamingos fit into the family tree of birds.

Grebes are freshwater diving birds. There are more than 20 species of grebes, including the great-crested grebe shown here.

A flock of flamingos feeds and rests in Lake Nakuru in Kenya, Africa.

Lagoon Life

Flamingos are choosy about where they live. Firstly, they don't like the cold, so they prefer to live in the tropics or subtropics. Secondly, they like to be near water that is salty, but not as salty as the sea. That is because the food flamingos like—small shrimplike animals and other tiny living things—live in semisalty, or **brackish**, water. This kind of water is found in marshes, swamps, and lagoons that are close to the sea, and also in some inland lakes.

Unfortunately, flamingos cannot drink brackish water. If they are thirsty, the birds have to go in search of freshwater, such as in a spring or a puddle left after it has rained. In fact, lesser flamingos are capable of standing in and drinking water from hot springs that is boiling hot—212°F (100°C)!

Filter Feeding

A flamingo's unusual beak serves a very important purpose. The beak filters out, or sifts, the small animals and other life-forms in the water. When feeding, a flamingo wades into the lake or lagoon and dips its head underwater. The bird then moves its head back and forth. Inside its beak, the bird moves its fleshy tongue back and forth, too. The action of the tongue draws water into the beak and pushes it out, over and over again. Lesser flamingos do that very fast—up to 20 times each second! Greater flamingos are slower at just four to five times a second.

The edges of the flamingo's beak—where the upper and lower parts meet—are lined with **bristles**. The bristles collect food as the water is pushed out. This way of collecting food is called **filter feeding**.

Greater flamingos have large bristles that collect animals up to 1 inch (2.5 cm) long, such as snails and water insects. Lesser flamingos have finer bristles suited to collecting microscopic food.

A bird's beak is made of
a tough substance called
keratin. Fingernails, horns,
hooves, feathers, and hair
are made of keratin, too.

A flamingo will even poke its beak into mud in an effort to find small animals.

Stir It Up!

A flamingo sometimes looks like it is dancing when it is feeding. As it swishes its head back and forth underwater, it stamps its webbed feet up and down.

In fact, the flamingo is stirring up the silty mud at the bottom of the shallow lake. That way, the food it eats—small animals and other tiny life-forms living in the mud—swirl around in the water. The flamingo can then easily filter them out.

Different types of flamingos sometimes feed side by side. They get along peacefully because they are not competing for the same food. Some flamingos prefer larger food that lives at the bottom of the lake. They dip their head deep down to the bottom. Other flamingos, including James's flamingos, prefer tiny life-forms that float near the lake's surface. Therefore, these birds dip their head just below the surface. The lower half of the beak of these flamingos is much deeper than that of bottom-feeders. It is suited to feeding close to the water's surface.

Pretty in Pink

All species of flamingos are some shade of pink. The greater flamingos that live in Africa and Asia are pale pink. They also have pink legs and feet. Their close relatives in the Caribbean are much brighter. Their upper feathers are crimson, and their underside is a paler shade of reddish pink. The only parts of an adult flamingo that are not a shade of pink are the black flight feathers, the black tip of the beak, and, in some species, the legs and feet.

It is the flamingo's diet that makes its feathers pink. The coloring comes from natural dyes, or **pigments**, in the food that the birds eat. Scientists only discovered that after flamingos in a zoo were given a different diet—not the food they would catch in the wild. These captive birds' feathers turned white!

Flamingos have excellent color vision. That allows them to appreciate one another's pink plumage.

Flamingos—and birds in general—are light compared to other animals of a similar size. That is mainly because most birds' bones are hollow.

Tall Birds

With their long legs and neck, flamingos are tall birds. The shortest member of the family is the lesser flamingo. It grows to 2⅔ feet (0.8 m) high and weighs up to 5½ pounds (2.5 kg). James's flamingo is about this size, too. Andean and Chilean flamingos are medium-sized flamingos. They reach about 4 feet (1.2 m) high. The greater flamingo is the tallest, measuring up to 4½ feet (1.4 m) high and weighing up to 8 pounds (3.5 kg). The adult males of all flamingo species are slightly larger than the adult females.

High Fliers

Flamingos have long, wide wings. The greater flamingo's wingspan is almost 5½ feet (1.7 m). Flamingos sometimes fly long distances. They can cover 370 miles (600 km) nonstop at speeds of up to 37 miles (60 km) per hour. They prefer to fly in cloudless skies with tailwinds to speed them along.

Flamingos are not that agile in the air. They cannot move their wings as quickly as birds with smaller wings. Therefore, flamingos cannot change directions easily. Their lack of aerobatic skill in flight makes them an easy target for large **birds of prey**, such as the fish eagle. To avoid ending up in the stomach of a **predator**, flamingos prefer to fly in the open after sunset, when most birds of prey have gone to sleep. If they do fly during the day, they either fly short distances or fly very high—again to avoid predators.

Flamingos have
black flight feathers.

If a flamingo's feathers are plucked or fall out, they lose their pink color.

22

Feathery Features

All birds have many things in common. They lay eggs, they have a beak, they have two legs and two wings—although not all of them can fly—and they have feathers. No other type of animal has feathers.

Most of a flamingo's feathers are **contour feathers**. Those give it a **streamlined** shape for flight. Contour feathers include long, stiff tail feathers, which allow a bird to steer in the air. They also include wing feathers, which allow a bird to fly, and the shorter feathers all over a flight bird's body.

The flamingo also has soft, fluffy feathers called **down**. These feathers trap a layer of air against the bird's body. That keeps the bird warm.

Shedding Feathers

Feathers can become battered and torn. When they do, they can no longer do their job properly—whether that is keeping the bird warm or helping it to fly. For that reason, birds shed their feathers from time to time and grow new ones. This process is called **molting**.

Most flamingos molt every year. Some molt twice a year. The first set of feathers is paler than the second set in birds that molt twice each year. Others molt every two years. Usually, a flamingo molts gradually, losing a few feathers here and there, and growing them back before others are shed. Occasionally, the bird might lose so many feathers at once that it cannot fly. The flamingo must then stay grounded until the flight feathers grow back. That is a dangerous time for the bird. Since it cannot fly away, it is then at greater risk from predators.

Keeping Clean

Flamingos, like all birds, spend a lot of time—up to one-third of their day—keeping their feathers in tiptop condition. Whenever flamingos find freshwater, they ruffle the long feathers of their wings and tail in the water to wash off dirt.

Flamingos produce a natural oil from a gland near the base of their tail. They use their beak to spread the oil over their feathers. This natural conditioner also keeps the feathers waterproof. Cleaning and oiling the feathers is known as **preening**.

The birds also use their beak to pick out any **parasites**, such as lice, living among the feathers. To scratch their head, flamingos sometimes use their feet!

Lesser flamingos
gather in flocks
of thousands.

On One Leg

When flamingos rest they usually do it standing on one leg in the shallows. They curl their neck around, and rest their head on their back or even under one of their wings.

This one-legged resting position is perfectly comfortable for the bird, and it is useful, too. By standing on just one foot—rather than both feet—the bird greatly reduces the amount of body heat lost to the cool water.

Flamingos also rest sitting down on land, especially when they are looking after their egg in the breeding season. They tend to sit facing into the wind, so their feathers do not get too ruffled.

There are 19 bones
in a flamingo's long,
flexible neck.

A group of flamingos performs a courtship dance. Flamingos have sharp eyesight, which allows them to stay in synch with one another.

Honks and Dances

Flamingos sound much like geese. They make honking calls, usually when in flight. At other times, the birds make different kinds of sounds. They might grunt and growl if threatened. During the breeding season, male flamingos honk and gabble to try to impress the females. If a female flamingo is impressed by a male, she returns his calls. The smitten pair then honk and gabble together.

Some flamingos perform courtship dances. They do these dances in an effort to impress one another. Groups of the birds run back and forth, holding their head as high as they can and turning it from side to side. Others honk loudly and flap their wings while stretching out their neck and cocking their tail. Another movement aimed to impress involves twisting the neck around and touching the body with the beak as though preening. Other flamingos only perform courtship dances after they have paired up.

Mud Nest

After the flamingos have paired up, they remain in their flocks. Each pair begins to build a nest in the shallow water or on mud flats. If they cannot find a suitable site, they sometimes nest on rocky islands in a lagoon or lake. A large group of breeding birds is called a **colony**.

Flamingos do not build nests from sticks and twigs with a soft lining of leaves like many other birds do. Instead, they build a cone-shaped mud structure with a flat top. The female flamingo chooses the site for the nest. She also does most of the building. She rakes up the mud with her beak, patting it every so often with her feet and beak to make sure it is sturdy. When the cone is about 12 to 16 inches (30 to 40 cm) high, her job is done.

A nest-building greater flamingo scoops up mud with its beak.

33

If a flamingo pair loses its egg, the female will usually lay another one.

34

Nest Complete!

The male flamingo adds the finishing touches to the mud nest. He hollows out the top to make a shallow bowl. That will stop the egg from rolling out when the female lays it. The pair also strengthen the base of the nest mound with pebbles, shells, grass, and more mud. A strong base protects the nest from being washed away. Flamingos that cannot find any mud to build their nest, use grass and gravel instead, often surrounding it with a layer of clay to keep it all together.

The nest is complete when the female lays her egg. Female flamingos usually lay one egg each breeding season. If the water level of the lagoon suddenly changes, the egg should still stay dry in its tall cone-shaped nest.

Eggs and Hatching

A flamingo's egg is chalky white in color. The parents take turns sitting on the egg to keep it warm. This process is called **incubation**. Every so often, one of the parents turns the egg. That makes sure the chick grows evenly and doesn't become stuck to the inside of the eggshell. Toward the end of its development inside the egg, the chick can hear its parents' calls. It soon learns to recognize their voices.

The chick is ready to **hatch** about a month after the female laid the egg. It makes "peep" noises as it begins to crack the shell. It uses a toothlike structure on the end of its beak to break through the shell. This "**egg tooth**" eventually falls off after the chick has hatched. The parents seem anxious as the chick hatches. They reply to the chick's calls with their own, encouraging it. It might take 24 to 36 hours for the chick to break out.

A newly hatched Caribbean flamingo chick takes a rest. Its damp down feathers dry in the sun.

A flamingo chick has gray eyes that turn yellow as the bird becomes older.

Curious Chick

A newly hatched flamingo chick looks quite different from an adult. It is covered in fluffy, pale gray down. Its beak is different. It is pink and straight. It will not start to develop its characteristic curve until the chick is a few weeks old. The chick's legs are swollen, too. The swelling gradually disappears over the first two days.

Within a week of hatching, the chick is ready to explore its surroundings. It takes a short walk away from the nest or even takes a swim in the lagoon or lake. Its parents follow, ready to defend their youngster from any danger.

Flamingo Milk

A flamingo chick has a special diet for the first month of its life—a red-colored "milk" that both parents produce. The milk is rich in proteins and fats. It is made by the lining of the upper **digestive tract**. To give the chick milk, the parent lowers its beak into the chick's upturned, open beak. The chick is always hungry, so both parents are kept busy feeding their youngster.

The chick grows fast on the nutritious milk. Within a few weeks, the chick's down is replaced with larger feathers. At this time, the beak also changes color and develops its downward curve.

A greater flamingo feeds its chick milk. Flamingo milk contains nutrients similar to those in mammals' milk.

A flamingo's most developed senses are vision and hearing. Their senses of smell and taste are poor.

Voice Recognition

A flamingo chick often loses its parents among the hundreds of other adults in the flock. In addition, the parents leave the chick every so often to filter feed. The chick will search for its parents among the flock. The little gray bird pecks at the legs of the adults, which are usually resting. The adult birds, disturbed from their rest, give a honk or a squawk. The chick listens attentively. The chick does not yet recognize its parents by how they look—it can only recognize them by their voice. The chick, like all flamingos, has very good hearing. Every flamingo sounds slightly different to the chick. Eventually it finds its mother or father.

In the Crèche

Like their parents, young flamingos like to be in flocks. The chicks seek out the company of other young flamingos. As soon as they can walk, the young gather in groups called **crèches** (KRESHIZ). These groups of young are always guarded by at least one set of parents, ready to protect them from any predators. A flamingo chick is a tasty snack for many predators, including fish eagles, hyenas, jackals, crocodiles, alligators, and even pigs! If a predator comes too close, the adult flamingos charge at it, flapping their strong wings and growling. That is usually enough to scare away most enemies.

Greater flamingo chicks wander among the tall legs of their parents in a colony in Africa.

45

Even though this Chilean flamingo chick can now filter feed, it still occasionally gets milk from its parents.

Growing Up

Chicks learn to fly at about three months old. By this age, they have grown their flight feathers. The young flamingos learn by watching and copying their parents and other adults. The young flamingos are a bit clumsy at first, but soon get the hang of taking off, turning in the air, and landing. The chicks have also learned to filter feed, too. They still stay close to their parents, though, for protection.

By the age of one year, young flamingos have a full set of pale feathers. It takes a couple more years, however, before they become completely pink. Flamingos reach full size by two years. They begin to breed at about the age of six years. Wild flamingos can live to 25 years or longer.

Flamingo Future

Flamingos have suffered from loss of **habitat** in many places. Areas where the birds breed have been drained or flooded, making the water levels unsuitable for raising chicks. Industries, such as mining, have also destroyed their habitat. Roads built near breeding grounds have scared away the birds or made it easier for predators to reach and attack the flamingos. In some places, flamingos' eggs are eaten by humans. The birds are also killed for their fat, which is used in traditional medicines. At one time, James's flamingo was thought to be **extinct**, but it was later rediscovered living alongside the Chilean flamingo.

Many zoos and bird parks across the world house flamingos as a popular attraction. In the wild, flamingos are now protected in many places, and none of the species is under threat of extinction. But the birds' habitats still need continued protection for the flamingo's future to be as rosy as its beautiful feathers.

Words to Know

Birds of prey   Birds such as eagles and hawks that hunt other animals.

Brackish   A word that describes water that is somewhat salty.

Bristles   Stiff hairlike structures.

Chick   A young bird.

Colony   A large group of nesting birds.

Contour feathers   Feathers that give a bird a streamlined shape for flight.

Crèches   Large groups of chicks, watched over by at least one pair of adult birds.

Digestive tract   The long passageway in the body through which food passes.

Down   Soft, fluffy feathers.

Egg tooth   A small toothlike structure on the tip of a chick's beak. The egg tooth is used to help the chick hatch.

Extinct   When all of a certain type of animal or plant are dead and gone forever.

Filter feeding	Sifting water to catch food. Flamingos filter feed using their beak.
Habitat	The type of place where an animal or plant lives.
Hatch	To emerge, or break out, of an egg.
Incubation	Sitting on an egg to keep it warm so the chick inside can develop.
Molting	Shedding old feathers and growing new ones.
Parasites	Tiny animals that live on or in another animal. Parasites feed on body tissues, such as blood and skin.
Pigments	Substances in an animal that give it a certain color or colors.
Plumage	Another word for feathers.
Predator	An animal that hunts other animals.
Preening	Cleaning and oiling the feathers.
Species	The scientific word for animals of the same kind that breed together.
Streamlined	A body shape that allows a bird to move easier through air when it is in flight.

Find Out More

Books

Romeu, E. *The Flamingo's Legs*. Animals of the Americas. Miami, Florida: Alfaguara, 2004.

Wicker, J. L. *Those Funny Flamingos*. Sarasota, Florida: Pineapple Press, 2004.

Web sites

Birds: Flamingo
www.sandiegozoo.org/animalbytes/t-flamingo.html
A lot of information about flamingos.

Greater Flamingo
animals.nationalgeographic.com/animals/birds/ greater-flamingo.html
A profile of the largest species of flamingo.

Index